The ESS  f

EUROPEAN HISTORY

1450 to 1648
The Renaissance, Reformation and the Wars of Religion

Allen Horstman, Ph.D.
Professor of History
Albion College
Albion, Michigan

K. M. W.

Research and Education Association
61 Ethel Road West
Piscataway, New Jersey 08854

THE ESSENTIALS ®
OF EUROPEAN HISTORY
1450 to 1648
The Renaissance and Reformation

Printed in the United States of America

Library of Congress Catalog Card Number 89-62456

International Standard Book Number 0-87891-706-3

ESSENTIALS is a registered trademark of
Research and Education Association, Piscataway, New Jersey 08854

What the "Essentials of History" Will Do for You

REA's "Essentials of History" series offers a new approach to the study of history that is different from what has been available previously. Each book in the series has been designed to steer a sensible middle course, by including neither too much nor too little information.

Compared with conventional history outlines, the "Essentials of History" offer far more detail, with fuller explanations and interpretations of historical events and developments. Compared with voluminous historical tomes and textbooks, the "Essentials of History" offer a far more concise, less ponderous overview of each of the periods they cover.

The "Essentials of History" are intended primarily to aid students in studying history, doing homework, writing papers and preparing for exams. The books are organized to provide quick access to information and explanations of the important events, dates, and persons of the period. The books can be used in conjunction with any text. They will save hours of study and preparation time while providing a firm grasp and insightful understanding of the subject matter.

Instructors too will find the "Essentials of History" useful. The books can assist in reviewing or modifying course outlines. They also can assist with preparation of exams, as well as serve as an efficient memory refresher.

In sum, the "Essentials of History" will prove to be handy reference sources at all times.

The authors of the series are respected experts in their fields. They present clear, well-reasoned explanations and interpretations of the complex political, social, cultural, economic and philosophical issues and developments which characterize each era.

In preparing these books REA has made every effort to assure their accuracy and maximum usefulness. We are confident that each book will prove enjoyable and valuable to its user.

Dr. Max Fogiel, Program Director

About the Author

Allen Horstman began his professional career as a lawyer after receiving his degree from Harvard Law School in 1968. Between 1973 and 1977, he earned both his M.A. and Ph.D. from the University of California, Berkeley. Since 1977, he has taught history at Albion College in Albion, Michigan, and currently holds the rank of professor.

Dr. Horstman was named a Visiting Research Fellow of the University of Bristol in 1983-4, and has twice been named as an American Bar Association Fellow, 1975-6 and 1983-4. He maintains memberships in the American Historical Association, the Conference of British Studies, the Midwestern Victorian Studies Association, the Indiana State Bar Association, Phi Alpha Theta, and the American Association of University Professors. He has published two books, *Victorian Divorce* and *The Federal Truth in Lending Law*, as well as numerous articles for magazines and journals.

CONTENTS

CHAPTER 1

THE LATE MIDDLE AGES

1.1 THEMES

The Middle Ages ("medieval" is the French word) were chronologically between the classical world of Greece and Rome and the modern world. The papacy and monarchs, after exercising much power and influence in the high Middle Ages, were in eclipse after 1300. During the late Middle Ages (1300 – 1500) all of Europe suffered from the Black Death. While in northern Europe England and France engaged in destructive warfare, in Italy the Renaissance had begun.

1.2 THE CHURCH

1.2.1 *Organization*

The church was a hierarchical or pyramidal organization with the believers at the base, who were ministered to by priests, who in turn were supervised by bishops – all under the leadership of the pope. Monks, nuns, and friars existed outside the pyramid but were usually governed by the pope as well.

1

1.2.2 Criticisms

In the late Middle Ages, numerous criticisms were directed against individuals and church practices, but not the idea of the church itself or Christian beliefs.

Corruption. Numerous decisions within the church's bureaucracy were influenced by money, friendship, or politics.

Simony. Simony – the purchase of church positions, such as a bishopric, rather than appointment to the positions based upon merit – was commonplace.

Pluralism. A man could hold more than one office in the church even though he would not be able to do both jobs at once. He might hire an assistant to do one of the jobs for him or it might be left undone. As he could not be both places, he was also open to the criticism of absenteeism.

1.2.3 Critics

These criticisms, and others such as those concerning extravagance, excessive wealth, political involvement, and sexual improprieties, were part of the hostility to the clergy called anticlericalism. Those who criticized were often attacked by the church as heretics

John Wycliff (1320 – 1384). An English friar who criticized the vices of the clergy, taxes collected by the pope, transubstantiation, and the authority of the pope. As he believed the church should follow only the Scriptures, he began translating the Bible from Latin into English. Wycliff's ideas were used by the peasants in the revolt of 1381, and his followers, Lollards, survived well into the fifteenth century.

John Huss (1369 – 1415). A Czech priest, with criticisms similar to Wycliff's, produced a national following in Bohemia which rejected the authority of the pope. Huss was burned at the stake at the Council of Constance.

1.2.4 Lay Piety

In the Rhine Valley of Germany mystics, such as Meister Eckhart (1260 – 1327) and Thomas a Kempis (1379 – 1471), sought direct knowledge of God through the realm of inner feelings, not observance of church rituals.

Gerard Groote (1340 – 1384) began a semi-monastic life for laymen in the Low Countries. The Brethren of the Common Life ran schools and led lives guided by the Christian principles of humility, tolerance, and love, all unconcerned with the roles of the institutional church.

1.2.5 Popes

The papacy, recognized as the leader of the western church since at least the thirteenth century, encountered a series of problems in the late Middle Ages which reduced the prestige of popes and interfered with their ability to deal with the problems underlying the criticisms.

Babylonian Captivity. In 1305, after a confrontation with the king of France, a new pope, Clement V was elected. He was a Frenchman and never went to Rome, settling instead in Avignon, near the French kingdom. While not held captive by the French kings, the popes in Avignon were seen as subservient to them. Also the atmosphere was one of luxury, and the popes concentrated on money and bureaucratic matters, not spiritual leadership. Popes resided in Avignon from 1309 to 1377.

Great Schism. In 1377 Pope Gregory XI returned to Rome, ending the Babylonian Captivity but soon died. Disputes over the election of his successor led to the election of two popes, one of whom stayed in Rome (Urban VI), the other (Clement VII) returning to Avignon. The monarchs chose different sides (England and Germany for Rome; France, Scotland, Aragon, Castile, Portugal, and Italian city-states for Avignon), while neither pope prosecuted any reforms of the church. The existence of two popes lasted until 1417.

Conciliar Movement. An effort was initiated to have the church ruled by, not the pope, but everyone in the church such as bishops, cardinals, theologians, abbots, and including laymen. The idea gained impetus from the existence of two popes and the abuses they were not correcting.

Marsiglio of Padua (1270 – 1342), author of *The Defender of the Peace,* argued that the church was subordinate to the state and that the church should be governed by a general council.

Efforts after 1409 by councils at Pisa (1409) and Constance (1414 – 8) united the church under one pope (Martin V) but failed to effect any reform of abuses, as all such efforts ended in struggles between the pope and councils over power in the church. Martin and his successors rejected the conciliar movement.

Renaissance Popes. After 1447, a series of popes encouraged and supported much artistic work in Rome. While their personal lives were often criticized for sexual laxness, these popes took more interest in political, military, and artistic activities than church reform. Sixtus IV (1471 – 84) started the painting of the Sistine Chapel which his nephew, Julius II (1503 – 13), whom Sixtus had promoted within the church, finished

4

with the employment of Michelangelo to paint the ceiling. Julius also successfully asserted his control over the Papal States in central Italy. These popes did not cause the Reformation, but they failed to do anything which might have averted it.

1.3   THE HUNDRED YEARS' WAR

The governments of Europe partially broke down in the late Middle Ages, as violence within and war without dominated the scene. Towards the end of the period monarchs began to reassert their power and control. The major struggle, between England and France, was the Hundred Years' War (1337 – 1453).

1.3.1   *Causes*

The English king was the vassal of the French king for the duchy of Aquitaine, and the French king wanted control of the duchy; this was the event that started the fighting. The English king, Edward III, had a claim to the French throne through his mother, a princess of France.

Additionally, French nobles sought opportunities to gain power at the expense of the French king. England also exported its wool to Flanders which was coming under control of the king of France.

Finally, kings and nobles shared the values of chivalry which portrayed war as a glorious and uplifting adventure.

1.3.2   *Course of the War*

The war was fought in France, though the Scots (with French encouragement) invaded northern England. Few major battles occurred — Crecy (1346), Poitiers (1356), Agincourt (1415) — which the English won due to the chivalrous excesses of the

FRANCE DURING
THE HUNDRED YEARS' WAR

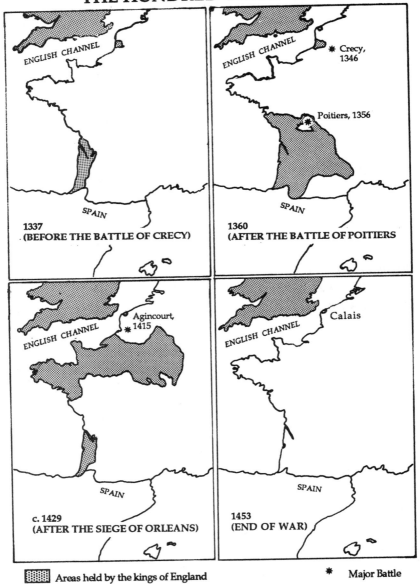

1337
(BEFORE THE BATTLE OF CRECY)

Crecy,
1346

Poitiers, 1356

1360
(AFTER THE BATTLE OF POITIERS

Agincourt,
1415

c. 1429
(AFTER THE SIEGE OF ORLEANS)

Calais

1453
(END OF WAR)

ENGLISH CHANNEL

SPAIN

▦ Areas held by the kings of England   ✱ Major Battle

French. The fighting consisted largely of sieges and raids. Eventually, the war became one of attrition; the French slowly wore down the English.

The technological changes during the war included the use of English longbows and the increasingly expensive plate armor of knights.

Joan of Arc (1412 – 1431). An illiterate peasant girl who said she heard voices of saints, Joan of Arc rallied the French army for several victories. Due to Joan's victories, Charles VII was crowned king at Rheims, the traditional location for enthronement. Joan was later captured by the Burgundians, allies of England, and sold to the English who tried her for heresy (witchcraft). She was burned her at the stake at Rouen.

1.3.3 *Results*

England lost all of its Continental possessions except Calais. French farmland was devastated and England and France both expended great sums of money. Population, especially in France, declined.

Both countries suffered internal disruption as soldiers plundered and local officials left to fight the war. Trade everywhere was disrupted and England's wool trade to the Low Countries slumped badly. To cover these financial burdens, heavy taxation was inflicted on the peasants.

Political changes occured in both countries:

England. The need for money led kings to summon parliaments more often which gave nobility and merchants more power. No taxes could be levied without parliamentary approval. Parliamentary procedures and institutions changed, giving nobles more control over government (impeachments). Representative government gained a tradition which enabled it to survive under later challenges.

A series of factional struggles led to the deposition of Richard II in 1399. After the Hundred Years' War ended the nobility continued fighting each other in the War of the Roses (1450 – 1485), choosing sides as Lancastrians and Yorkists.

France. Noble factions contended for power with the king, who refused to deal with noble assemblies. The king faced various problems, while holding certain advantages:

1) The Duchy of Burgundy was virtually independent.

2) There was no national assembly to confront, but only a series of provincial bodies.

3) The monarch had the right to levy a tax on salt, the *gabelle*, and a national tax, the *taille*, which exempted nobles and clergy.

4) A royal standing army existed so reliance on nobles became unnecessary.

In both countries the war led to the growth of nationalism, the feeling of unity among the subjects of a country:

1) Kings in both countries used propaganda to rally popular support.

2) Hatred of the enemy united people.

3) Military accomplishments fed national pride.

Literature also came to express nationalism, as it was written in the language of the people instead of Latin. Geoffrey Chaucer (1340 – 1400) portrayed a wide spectrum of English life in the *Cantebury Tales*, while Francois Villon (1431 – 1463), in his *Grand Testament*, emphasized the ordinary life of the French with humor and emotion.

1.4 THE HOLY ROMAN EMPIRE

After prolonged struggles with the papacy in the thirteenth century, the Holy Roman Emperor had little power in either Germany or Italy. After 1272, the empire was usually ruled by a member of the Hapsburg family which had turned its interest to creating possessions in Austria and Hungary. The Ottoman Turks, following the conquest of Constantinople in 1453, continually pressed on the borders of the Empire.

In 1356 the Golden Bull was issued. This constitution of the empire gave the right of naming the emperor to seven German electors, but gave the pope no role.

The Swiss cantons gradually obtained independence, helped by stories such as that of William Tell.

In Italy, city-states, or communes, dominated by wealthy merchants, continued their efforts to obtain independence of the emperor.

In many cities, the governments became stronger and were dominated by despots (Milan had the Visconti and later the Sforza; Florence came under the control of the Medici) or oligarchies (Venice was ruled by the Council of Ten). Other smaller city-states disappeared as continual wars led to larger territories dominated by one large city.

1.5   THE NEW MONARCHS

After 1450, monarchs turned to strengthening their power internally, a process producing the "New Monarchy."

1.5.1   *Problems*

Money. The general economic stagnation of the late Middle Ages combined with the increasing expense of mercenary armies to force monarchs to seek new taxes, something traditionally requiring the consent of the nobles.

Nobles. Long the chief problem for kings, nobles faced declining incomes and rising desires to control the government of their king. If not fighting external foes, they engaged in civil war at home with their fellow nobles.

Unfortunately for the monarchs, many weak, incompetent or insane kings hindered their efforts.

1.5.2   *Opposition to Monarchian Power*

Nobles claimed various levels of independence under feudal rules or traditions. Forming an assembly provided some sort of a meeting forum for nobles. Furthermore, the core of royal armies consisted of nobles; monarchs were solaced only by the appearance of mercenary armies of pike which reduced royal reliance on noble knights. Many of the higher clergy of the church were noble born.

Additionally, some towns had obtained independence during times of trouble. Church and clergy saw the pope as their leader.

THE CHRISTIAN CONQUEST OF SPAIN

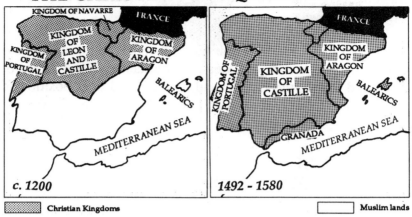

| Christian Kingdoms | Muslim lands |

1.5.3 *Help for France's Monarchy*

The defeat of the English in the Hundred Years' war removed the external threat. The defeat of the duchy of Burgundy in 1477 removed a major military power holding part of eastern France. Trade was expanded, fostered by the merchant Jacques Coeur (1395 – 1456). Louis XI (1461 – 1483) demonstrated ruthlessness in dealing with his nobility as individuals and collectively in the Estates-General.

1.5.4 *Help for England's Monarchy*

Many nobles died in the War of the Roses. Nobles were controlled by a royal court, the Star Chamber. Standard governmental procedures of law and taxation were developed.

1.5.5 *Help for Spain's Monarchy*

The marriage of Isabella of Castile (1474 – 1504) and Ferdinand of Aragon (1478 – 1516) created a united Spain. Navarre was conquered in 1512. Moslems were defeated at Granada in 1492.

Additionally, sheep farming was encouraged through a government organization, the Mesta. An alliance with a group of cities and towns, the Hermandad, was formed in opposition of the nobility. Finally, reform and control of the church was enacted through the Inquisition.

1.6 THE BLACK DEATH AND SOCIAL PROBLEMS

The bubonic plague ("Black Death") is a disease affecting the lymph glands and causes death quickly. Existing conditions in Europe encouraged the quick spread of disease:

1) There was no urban sanitation, and streets were filled with refuse, excrement and dead animals.

2) Houses were made of wood, clay and mud with straw roofs.

3) Living conditions were overcrowded, with families often sleeping in one room or one bed.

4) Poor nutrition was rampant, due to population pressures on food supplies.

5) There was a general lack of personal cleanliness.

Carried by fleas on black rats, the plague was brought from Asia by merchants and arrived in Europe in 1347. The plague affected all of Europe by 1350 and killed perhaps 25 to 40 percent of the population, with cities suffering more than the countryside.

1.6.1 Consequences

Some of the best clergy died because they attempted to help the sick; the church was left to the less competent or sincere. With fewer people, the economy declined.

A general pessimism pervaded the survivors. Flagellants whipped and scourged themselves in penance for sins which they believed caused the plague. Literature and art reflected this attitude, including such examples as the Dance of Death, which depicted dancing skeletons among the living.

Additionally, Jews were killed due to a belief that they poisoned wells of Christians.

1.6.2 Population

By 1300, Europe's population had reached the limit of available food resources and famines became common. A series of consequences manifested after the decline of population after 1350:

1) Wages became higher as the remaining workers could obtain better wages or move; governments often responded with laws trying to set wage levels, such as England's Statute of Laborers (1351).

2) Serfdom ended in many places.

3) Guilds were established which limited membership and cities limited citizenship in efforts to obtain or protect monopolies. The Hanseatic League of German cities controlled the Baltic trade in the fourteenth and early fifteenth centuries.

4) Sheep farming increased, as sheep needed fewer workers and the necessary enclosures of open fields in England eliminated peasants and their villages.

1.6.3 *Peasant Revolts*

Records do not reveal major peasant revolts prior to the thirteenth century. New conditions following the Plague led to increased revolutionary activity:

1) Taxation was increased due to the Hundred Years' War.

2) Higher wages were desired after the Black Death.

3) Rising expectations were frustrated after a period of relative prosperity.

4) Hostility to aristocrats increased, as expressed in the words of a priest, John Ball, one of the leaders of the English Peasants' Revolt: "When Adam delved and Eve span / Who was then the gentleman?"

A number of subsequent revolts ensued:

1) In England, the largest of these, the Peasants' Revolt of 1381, involved perhaps 100,000 people.

2) France experienced The *Jacquerie* in 1358.

3) Poor workers revolted in Florence in 1378.

The Low Countries, Germany, Sicily, Spain, and at other times in England and France all experienced similar occurences.

CHAPTER 2

THE RENAISSANCE

2.1 THEMES

The Renaissance occurred mainly in Italy between the years 1300 and 1600. New learning and changes in styles of art were two of the most pronounced characteristics of the Renaissance. The Renaissance contrasts with the Middle Ages:

1) The Renaissance was secular, not religious.

2) The individual, not the group, was emphasized during the Renaissance.

3) The Renaissance occurred in urban, not rural, areas.

Italian city-states, such as Venice, Milan, Padua, Pisa, and especially Florence were the home to most Renaissance developments, which were limited to the rich elite.

Jacob Burckhardt, in *The Civilization of the Renaissance in Italy* (1860), popularized the study of the period and argued that it was a strong contrast with the Middle Ages. Subsequent historians have often found more continuity with the Middle Ages in terms of the society and its traditions. Whether the term applies to a cultural event or merely a time period is still debated.

2.2 DEFINITIONS

Renaissance – French for 'rebirth'; the word describes the reawakening, rebirth, of interest in the heritage of the classical past.

Classical past – Greece and Rome in the years between 500 B.C. and 400 A.D. Humanist scholars were most interested in Rome from 200 B.C. to 180 A.D.

Humanism – The reading and understanding of writings and ideals of the classical past. Rhetoric was the initial area of study which soon widened to include poetry, history, politics, and philosophy. Civic humanism was the use of humanism in the political life of Italian city-states. Christian humanism focused on early Church writings instead of secular authors.

Individualism – Behavior or theory which emphasizes each person and is contrasted with corporate or community behavior or theory in which the group is emphasized at the expense of the individual. Renaissance individualism sought great accomplishments and looked for heroes of history.

Virtu – The essence of being a person by showing human abilities. This ability could be displayed in speech, art, politics, warfare, or elsewhere by seizing the opportunities available. For many, the pursuit of virtu was amoral.

Florentine or Platonic Academy – located in a country house and supported by the Medici, the leading Florentine political family, a group of scholars who initially studied the works of Plato, the ancient Greek. The leading members were Marsilio Ficino (1433 – 1499) and Pico della Mirandola (1463 – 1494).

2.3 CAUSES

While no cause can be clearly identified as the source for the Renaissance, several categories have been suggested by historians:

Economic. Northern Italy was very wealthy as a result of serving as intermediary between the silk- and spice-producing East and the consuming West of England, France and Germany. Also, Italian merchants had built great wealth in the cloth industry and had often turned to international banking. This wealth gave people leisure to pursue new ideas and money to support the artists and scholars who produced the new works.

Political. Struggles between the papacy, the Holy Roman Empire, and merchants during the Middle Ages had resulted in the independence of many small city-states in northern Italy. This fragmentation meant no single authority had the power to stop or redirect new developments. The governments of the city-states, often in the hands of one man, competed by supporting artists and scholars.

Historical. Northern Italy cities were often built on the ruins of ancient Roman ones, and the citizens knew of their heritage.

Ideas. The appearance of men fleeing the falling Byzantine

Empire brought new ideas, including the study of Greek, to Italy. Also, during the numerous wars between the Italian city-states, contestants sought justifications for their claims in the actions of the past, even back to the classical past. Finally, the study of Roman law during disputes between the popes and the Holy Roman Emperors led to study of other Roman writers.

2.4 LITERATURE, ART, AND SCHOLARSHIP

2.4.1 *Literature*

Humanists, as both orators and poets, were inspired by and imitated works of the classical past. The literature was more secular and covered more subjects than that of the Middle Ages.

Dante (1265 – 1321), a Florentine writer who spent much of his life in exile after being on the losing side in political struggles in Florence. His *Divine Comedy*, describing a journey through hell, purgatory, and heaven, shows that reason can only take people so far and then God's grace and revelation must be used. Dealing with many other issues and with much symbolism, the work is the pinnacle of medieval poetry.

Petrarch (1304 – 1374) wrote in both Latin and Italian, encouraged the study of ancient Rome, collected and preserved much work of ancient writers, and produced much work in the classical literary style. He is best known for his sonnets, including many expressing his love for a married woman named Laura, and is considered the father of humanism.

Boccaccio (1313 – 1375) wrote *The Decameron*, a collection of short stories in Italian, which meant to amuse, not edify, the reader.

Castiglione (1478 – 1529), authored *The Book of the Courtier* which specified the qualities necessary for a gentleman – including the development of both intellectual and physical qualities – and who will lead an active, non-contemplative life. Abilities in conversation, sports, arms, dance, music, Latin and Greek should be combined with an agreeable personal demeanor. The book was translated into many languages and greatly influenced Western ideas about correct education and behavior.

2.4.2 Art

Artists also broke with the medieval past, in both technique and content.

Painting. Medieval painting, usually depicting religious topics and for religious uses, was idealized, and portrayed the essence or idea of the topic. Renaissance art sometimes used religious topics, but often dealt with secular themes or portraits of individuals. Oil paints, chiaroscuro, and linear perspectives all combined to produce works of energy in three dimensions.

Sculpture. Medieval sculpture was dominated by works of religious significance. The idealized forms of individuals, such as saints, were often used in the education of the faithful who could not easily deal with concepts. By copying classical models and using free standing pieces, Renaissance sculptors produced works celebrating the individualistic and non-religious spirit of the day.

Architecture. Medieval architecture included the use of pointed arches, flying buttresses, and fan vaulting to obtain great heights while permitting light to flood the interior of the building, usually a church or cathedral. The result gave a 'feeling' for God rather than the approach through reach. The busy details, filling every niche, and the absence of of symmetry also typify medieval work.

Renaissance architects openly copied classical, especially Roman, forms, such as the rounded arch and squared angles, while constructing town and country houses for the rich and urban buildings for cities.

Several artists became associated with the new style or art:

Giotto (1266 – 1336) painted religious scenes using light and shadow, a technique called chiaroscuro, to create an illusion of depth and greater realism. He is considered the father of Renaissance painting.

Donatello (1386 – 1466), the father of Renaissance sculpture, produced, in his *David*, the first statue cast in bronze since classical times.

Masaccio (1401 – 1428) emphasized naturalism in *Expulsion of Adam and Eve* by showing real human figures, in the nude, with three-dimensions, expressing emotion.

Leonardo de Vinci (1452 – 1519), produced numerous works, including *Last Supper* and *Mona Lisa*, as well as many mechanical designs, though few were ever constructed.

Raphael (1483 – 1520), a master of Renaissance grace and style, theory and technique, represented these skills in *The School of Athens*.

Michelangelo (1475 – 1564), a universal man, produced masterpieces in architecture, sculpture (*David*), and painting (the Sistine Chapel ceiling). His work was a bridge to new, non-Renaissance style called Mannerism.

2.4.3 Scholars

Scholars sought to know what is good and to practice it, as

men in the Middle Ages. However, Renaissance people sought more practical results and did not judge things by religious standards. Manuscript collections enabled scholars to study the primary sources they used and to reject all traditions which had been built up since classical times. Also, scholars participated in the lives of their cities as active politicians.

Leonardo Bruni (1370 – 1444), civic humanist, served as chancellor of Florence where he used his rhetorical skills to rouse the citizens against external enemies. He also wrote a history of his city and was the first to use the term humanism.

Lorenzo Valla (1407 – 1457), authored *Elegances of the Latin Language*, the standard text in Latin philology, and also exposed the Donation of Constantine, which purported to give the Papacy control of vast lands in Italy, as a forgery.

Machiavelli (1469 – 1527), wrote *The Prince*, and analyzed politics from the standpoint of reason, not faith or tradition. His work, amoral in tone, describes how a political leader could obtain and hold power by acting only in his own self interest.

2.5   THE RENAISSANCE OUTSIDE ITALY

The Renaissance in the rest of western Europe was less classical in its emphasis as well as more influenced by religion. Christian humanism, the application of humanist approaches to Christianity, is discussed in 2.6.

The Low Countries. Artists still produced works on religious themes but the attention to detail in the paintings of Jan van Eyck (1385 – 1440) typifies Renaissance ideas. Later artists include the nearly surreal Pieter Brueghel (1520 – 1569) and Rembrandt van Rijn (1606 – 1669).

Germany. The invention at Mainz around 1450 of printing with movable type, traditionally attributed to Johann Gutenberg, enabled new ideas to be spread throughout Europe more easily. Albrecht Durer (1471 – 1528) gave realism and individuality to the art of the woodcut.

France. Many Italian artists and scholars were hired. The Loire Valley chateaux of the sixteenth century and Rabelais' (1494 – 1553) *Gargantua and Pantagruel* reflect Renaissance tastes.

England. Interests in the past and new developments did not appear until the sixteenth century. Drama, culminating in the age of Shakespeare, is the most pronounced accomplishment of the Renaissance spirit in England.

Spain. Money from the American conquests supported much building, such as the Escoral, a palace and monastery, and art, such as that by El Greco (1541 – 1614), who is often considered to work in the style of Mannerism.

2.6   CHRISTIAN HUMANISM

2.6.1   *Theme*

Much of the Renaissance outside Italy focused on religious matters by studying the writings of the early Christian church, rather than the secular authors of Rome and Greece.

2.6.2   *Elements*

Although they used the techniques of the Italian humanists in the analysis of ancient writings, language and style, Christian humanists were more interested in providing guidance on personal behavior.

The work on Christian sources, done between 1450 and 1530, emphasized education and the power of the human intellect to bring about institutional change and moral improvement. The many tracts and guides of Christian humanists were directed at reforming the church but led many into criticisms of the church which resulted in the Reformation. Additionally, the discovery that traditional Christian texts had different versions proved unsettling to many believers.

Though many Christian humanists were not clergymen, most early reformers of the church during the Reformation had been trained as Christian humanists.

Christian Humanism, with its emphasis on toleration and education, disappeared due to the increasing passions of the Reformation after 1530.

2.6.3 Biographies

Desiderius Erasmus (1466 – 1536), a Dutchman and the most notable figure of the Christian humanist movement, made new translations of the Greek and Latin versions of the New Testament in order to have 'purer' editions. His book *In Praise of Folly* satirizes the ambitions of the world, most especially those of the clergy. A man known throughout the intellectual circles of Europe, he emphasized the virtues of tolerance, restraint, and education at the time the church was fragmenting during the Reformation. Erasmus led a life of simple piety, practicing the Christian virtues, which led to complaints that he had no role for the institutional church. His criticisms of the church and clergy, though meant to lead to reforms, gave ammunition to those wishing to attack the church and, therefore, it is said "Erasmus laid the egg that Luther hatched."

Thomas More (1478 – 1536), an English laywer, politician, and humanist, wrote *Utopia* (a Greek word for 'nowhere').

Mixing civic humanism with religious ideals, the book describes a perfect society, located on an imaginary island, in which war, poverty, religious intolerance, and other problems of the early sixteenth century do not exist. *Utopia* sought to show how people might live if they followed the social and political ideals of Christianity. Also, in a break with medieval thought, More portrayed government as very active in the economic life of the society, education, and public health. Though a critic of the church and clergy of his day, More was executed by Henry VIII, king of England, for refusing to countenance Henry's break with the pope in religious matters.

Jacques Lefevre d'Etables (1454 − 1536), the leading French humanist, produced five versions of the Psalms, his *Quincuplex Psalterism*, which challenged the belief in the tradition of a single, authoritative Bible. Also, his work on St. Paul anticipated that of Luther.

Francesco Ximenes de Cisneros (1436 − 1517), leader of the Spanish church as Grand Inquisitor, founded a university and produced the *Complutensian Polyglot Bible*, which had Hebrew, Greek, and Latin versions of the Bible in parallel columns. He also reformed the Spanish clergy and church so that most criticisms of the later reformers during the Reformation did not apply to Spain.

CHAPTER 3

THE REFORMATION

3.1 THEMES

The Reformation destroyed Western Europe's religious unity, involved new ideas about the relationships among God, the individual, and society, had its course greatly influenced by politics, and led, in most areas, to the subjection of the church to the political rulers.

3.2 BACKGROUND

Earlier threats to the unity of the church had been made by the works of John Wycliff and John Huss. The abuses of church practices and positions upset many people. Likewise, Christian humanists had been criticizing the abuses.

Personal piety and mysticism, alternative approaches to Christianity, which did not require the apparatus of the institutional church and the clergy, had been appearing in the late Middle Ages.

3.3   MARTIN LUTHER (1483 – 1546) AND THE BEGINNINGS

3.3.1   *Personal Background*

Martin Luther was miner's son from Saxony in central Germany. At the urgings of his father, he studied for a career in law. He underwent a religious experience while traveling, which led him to become an Augustinian friar. Later, he became a professor at the university in Wittenberg, Saxony.

3.3.2   *Religious Problems*

Luther, to his personal distress, could not reconcile the problem of the sinfulness of the individual and the justice of God. How could a sinful person attain the righteousness necessary to obtain salvation? During his studies of the Bible, especially of Romans 1:17, Luther came to believe that personal efforts – good works such as a Christian life and attention to the sacraments of the church – could not 'earn' the sinner salvation but that belief and faith were the only way to obtain grace. "Justification by faith alone" was the road to salvation, Luther believed by 1515.

3.3.3   *Indulgences*

Indulgences, which had originated in connection with the Crusades, involved the cancellation of the penalty given by the church to a confessed sinner. Indulgences had long been a means of raising money for church activities. In 1517, the pope was building the new cathedral of St. Peter in Rome. Also, Albrecht, Archbishop of Mainz, had purchased three church positions (simony and pluralism) by borrowing money from the banking family, the Fuggers. A Dominican friar, John Tetzel, was authorized to preach and sell indulgences, with the proceeds going to build the cathedral and repay the loan. The popular belief was that "As soon as a coin in the coffer rings, the soul from purgatory springs," and Tetzel had much business. On October 31, 1517, Luther, with his belief that no such control or influence could be had over salvation, nailed 95 theses, or statements, about indulgences to the door of the Wittenberg church and challenged the practice of selling indulgences. At this time he was seeking to reform the church, not divide it.

3.3.4 Luther's Relations with the Pope and Governments

In 1519 Luther debated various criticisms of the church and was driven to say that only the Bible, not religious traditions or papal statements, could determine correct religious practices and beliefs. In 1521 Pope Leo X excommunicated Luther for his beliefs.

In 1521 Luther appeared in the city of Worms before a meeting (Diet) of the important figures of the Holy Roman Empire, including the Emperor, Charles V. He was again condemned. At the Diet of Worms Luther made his famous statement about his writings and the basis for them: "Here I stand. I can do no other." After this, Luther could not go back; the break with the pope was permanent.

Frederick III of Saxony, the ruler of the territory in which Luther resided, protected Luther in Wartburg Castle for a year. Frederick never accepted Luther's beliefs but protected him because Luther was his subject. The weak political control of the Holy Roman Emperor contributed to Luther's success in avoiding the penalties of the pope and the Emperor.

3.3.5 Luther's Writings

An Address to the Christian Nobility of the German Nation (1520) argued that nobles, as well as clergy, were the leaders of the church and should undertake to reform it.

The Babylonian Captivity (1520) attacked the traditional seven sacraments, replacing them with only two.

The Freedom of the Christian Man (1520) explains Luther's views on faith, good works, the nature of God, and the supremacy of political authority over believers.

Against the Murderous, Thieving Hordes of the Peasants (1524), written in response to the Peasants' Revolt, stated Luther's belief that political leaders, not all people, should control both church and society.

By 1534 Luther translated the Bible into German, making it accessible to many more people as well as greatly influencing the development of the German language. Also, his composition, "A Mighty Fortress is Our God," was the most popular hymn of the sixteenth century. The printing press enabled Luther's works to be distributed quickly throughout Germany.

3.3.6 *Subsequent Developments of Lutheranism*

Economic burdens being increased on the peasants by their lords, combined with Luther's words that a Christian is subject to no one, led the peasants of Germany to revolt in 1524. The ensuing noble repression, supported by Luther, resulted in the deaths of 70,000 to 100,000 peasants.

At a meeting of the Holy Roman Empire's leading figures in 1529, a group of rulers, influenced by Luther's teachings "protested" the decision of the majority – hence the term "Protestant." Protestant originally meant Lutheran but eventually was applied to all Western Christians who did not maintain allegiance to the pope.

After a failure of Protestant and Catholic representatives to find a mutually acceptable statement of faith, the Augsburg Confession of 1530 was written as a comprehensive statement of Lutheran beliefs.

Led by Philip Melanchthon (1497 – 1560), the "Educator of Germany," Lutherans undertook much educational reform, including schools for girls.

Denmark became Lutheran in 1523 and Sweden in 1527.

Lutheran rulers, to protect themselves against the efforts of Charles V, the Holy Roman Emperor, to reestablish Catholicism in Germany, formed a defensive alliance at Schmalkald, the Schmalkaldic League, in 1531.

Wherever Lutheranism was adopted, church lands were often seized by the ruler. This made a return to Catholicism more difficult, as the lands would need to be restored to the church.

After warfare in the 1540's, which Charles V won but was unable to follow up because his treatment of defeated political rulers in Germany offended the nobility of the Empire, the Peace of Augsburg (1555) established the permanent religious division of Germany into Lutheran and Catholic churches. The statement *"cuius regio, eius religio"* ("whose region, his religion") meant that the religion of any area would be that of the ruling political authority.

3.4   OTHER REFORMERS

Martin Luther was not so much the father as the elder brother of the Reformation because many other reformers were criticizing the church by the early 1520's.

3.4.1 *Ulrich Zwingli*

Ulrich Zwingli (1484 – 1531) introduced reforming ideas in Zurich in Switzerland. He rejected clerical celibacy, the worship of saints, fasting, transubstantiation, and purgatory. Rejecting ritual and ceremony, Zwingli stripped churchs of decorations, such as statues. In 1523 the governing council of the city accepted his beliefs. Zurich became a center for Protestantism and its spread throughout Switzerland.

Zwingli, believing in the union of church and state, established in Zurich a system which required church attendance by all citizens and regulated many aspects of personal behavior – all enforced by courts and a group of informers.

Efforts to reconcile the views of Zwingli and Luther, chiefly over the issue of the Eucharist, failed during a meeting in Marburg Castle in 1529.

Switzerland, divided into many cantons, also divided into Protestant and Catholic camps. A series of civil wars, during which Zwingli was captured and executed, led to a treaty in which each canton was permitted to determine its own religion.

3.4.2 *Anabaptists*

Anabaptist (derived from a Greek word meaning to baptize again) is a name applied to people who rejected the validity of child baptism and believed that such children had to be rebaptized when they became adults.

As the Bible became available, through translation into the languages of the people, many people adopted interpretations contrary to those of Luther, Zwingli, and the Catholics.

Anabaptists sought to return to the practices of the early Christian church, which was a voluntary association of believers with no connection to the state. Perhaps the first Anabaptists appeared in Zurich in 1525 under the leadership of Conrad Grebel (1498 – 1526), and were called Swiss Brethren.

In 1534, a group of Anabaptists, called Melchiorites, led by Jan Matthys, gained political control of the city of Munster in Germany and forced other Protestants and Catholics to convert or leave. Most of the Anabaptists were workers and peasants, and the city then followed Old Testament practices, including polygamy, and abolished private property. Combined armies of Protestants and Catholics captured the city and executed the leaders in 1535. Thereafter, Anabaptism and Munster became stock words of other Protestants and Catholics about the dangers of letting reforming ideas influence workers and peasants.

Subsequently, Anabaptists adopted pacifism and avoided involvement with the state whenever possible. Today, the Mennonites, founded by Menno Simons (1496 – 1561), and the Amish are the descendents of the Anabaptists.

3.4.3 *John Calvin*

John Calvin (1509 – 1564), a Frenchman, arrived in Geneva, a Swiss city-state which had adopted an anti-Catholic position, in 1536 but failed in his first efforts to further the reforms. Upon his return in 1540, Geneva became the center of the Reformation. Calvin's *Institutes of the Christian Religion* (1536), a strictly logical analysis of Christianity, had a universal, not local or national, appeal.

Calvin brought knowledge of organizing a city from his stay in Strasbourg, which was being led by the reformer Martin Bucer (1491 – 1551). Calvin differed from Luther as Calvin emphasized the doctrine of predestination (God knew who would obtain salvation before those people were born) and believed that church and state should be united.

As in Zurich, church and city combined to enforce Christian behavior, and Calvinism came to be seen as having a stern morality. Like Zwingli, Calvin rejected most aspects of the medieval church's practices and sought a simple, unadorned church. Followers of Calvinism became the most militant and uncompromising of all Protestants.

Geneva became the home to Protestant exiles from England, Scotland, and France, who later returned to their countries with Calvinist ideas.

Calvinism ultimately triumphed as the majority religion in Scotland, under the leadership of John Knox (1505 – 1572), and the United Provinces of the Netherlands. Puritans in England and New England also accepted Calvinism.

3.5 REFORM IN ENGLAND

England underwent reforms in a pattern differing from the rest of Europe. Personal and political decisions by the rulers determined much of the course of the Reformation there.

3.5.1 *The Break with the Pope*

Henry VIII (1509 – 1547) married Katherine of Aragon, the widow of his older brother. By 1526 Henry became convinced that his inability to produce a legitimate son to inherit his throne was because he had violated God's commandments (Leviticus 18:16, 20:21) by marrying his brother's widow.

Soon, Henry fell in love with Anne Boleyn and decided to annul his marriage to Katherine in order to marry Anne. The pope, Clement VII, the authority necessary to issue such an annulment was, after 1527, under the political control of Charles V, Katherine's nephew. Efforts to secure the annulment, directed by Cardinal Wolsey (1474 – 1530) ended in failure and Wolsey's disgrace. Thomas Cranmer (1489 – 1556), named archbishop in 1533, dissolved Henry's marriage, which permitted him to marry Anne Boleyn in January 1533.

Henry used Parliament to threaten the pope and eventually to legislate the break with Rome by law. The *Act of Annates* (1532) prevented payments of money to the pope. The *Act of Restraint of Appeals* (1533) forbade appeals to be taken to Rome, which stopped Katherine from appealing her divorce to the pope. The *Act of Supremacy* (1534) which declared Henry, not the pope, as the head of the English church. Subsequent acts enabled Henry to dissolve the monasteries and to seize their land, which represented perhaps 25% of the land of England.

In 1536, Thomas More was executed for rejecting Henry's leadership of the English church.

Protestant beliefs and practices made little headway during Henry's reign as he accepted transubstantiation, enforced celibacy among the clergy and otherwise made the English church conform to most medieval practices.

3.5.2 *Protestantism*

Under Henry VIII's son, Edward VI (1547 – 1553), a child of ten at his accession, the English church adopted Calvinism. Clergy were allowed to marry, communion by the laity expanded, and images were removed from churches. Doctrine included justification by faith, the denial of transubstantiation, and only two sacraments.

3.5.3 *Catholicism*

Under Mary (1553 – 1558), Henry VII's daughter and half-sister of Edward VI, Catholicism was restored and England reunited with the pope. Over 300 people were executed, including bishops and Archbishop Cranmer, for refusing to abandon their Protestant beliefs. Numerous Protestants fled to the Continent where they learned of more advanced Protestant beliefs, including Calvinism at Geneva.

3.5.4 *Anglicanism*

Under Elizabeth (1558 – 1603), Henry VII's daughter and half-sister of Edward and Mary, the church in England adopted Protestant beliefs again. The *Elizabethan Settlement* required outward conformity to the official church but rarely inquired about inward beliefs.

Some practices of the church, including ritual, resembled the Catholic practices. Catholicism remained, especially among the gentry, but could not be practiced openly.

Some reformers wanted to purify (hence "Puritans") the church of its remaining Catholic aspects. The resulting church, Protestant in doctrine and practice but retaining most of the physical possessions, such as buildings, and many powers, such as church courts, of the medieval church, was called Anglican.

3.6 REFORM ELSEWHERE IN EUROPE

3.6.1 *Ireland*

The Parliament in Ireland established a Protestant church much like the one in England. The landlords and people near Dublin were the only ones who followed their monarchs into

Protestantism as the mass of the Irish people were left untouched by the Reformation. The Catholic church and its priests became the religious, and eventually the national, leaders of the Irish people.

3.6.2 *Scotland*

John Knox (1505 – 72), upon his return from the Continent, led the Reformation in Scotland. Parliament, dominated by nobles, established Protestantism in 1560. The resulting church was Calvinist in doctrine.

3.6.3 *France*

France, near Geneva and Germany, experienced efforts at establishing Protestantism, but the kings of France had control of the church there and gave no encouragement to reformers. Calvinists, known in France as Huguenots, were especially common among the nobility and, after 1562, a series of civil wars involving religious differences resulted.

3.6.4 *Spain*

The church in Spain, controlled by the monarchy, allowed no Protestantism to take root. Similarly Italian political authorities rejected Protestantism.

3.7 THE COUNTER REFORMATION

The Counter Reformation brought changes to the portion of the Western church which retained its allegiance to the pope. Some historians see this as a reform of the Catholic church, similar to what Protestants were doing, while other see it as a result of the criticisms of Protestants.

Efforts to reform the church were given new impetus by Luther's activities. These included new religious orders such as Capuchins (1528), Theatines (1534) and Ursulines (1535), as well as mystics such as Teresa of Vaila (1515 – 1582).

Ignatius of Loyola (1491 – 1556), a former soldier, founded the Society of Jesus in 1540 to lead the attack on Protestantism. Jesuits, trained pursuant to ideas found in Ignatius' *Spiritual Exercises*, had dedication and determination and became the leaders in the Counter Reformation. In addition to serving in Europe, by the 1540's Jesuits, including Francies Xavier (1506 – 1552), traveled to Japan as missionaries.

Popes resisted reforming efforts because of fears as to what a council of church leaders might do to papal powers. The Sack of Rome in 1527, when soldiers of the Holy Roman Emperor captured and looted Rome, was seen by many as a judgment of God against the lives of the Renaissance popes. In 1534, Paul III became pope and attacked abuses while reasserting papal leadership.

Convened by Paul III and firmly under papal control, the Council of Trent met in three sessions from 1545 to 1563. It settled many aspects of doctrine including transubstantiation, the seven sacraments, the efficacy of good works for salvation, and the role of saints and priests. It also approved the "Index of Forbidden Books."

Other reforms came into effect. The sale of church offices was curtailed. New seminaries for more and better trained clergy were created. The revitalized Catholic church, the papacy, and the Jesuits set out to reunite Western Christianity.

Individuals who adopted other views but who had less impact on large groups of people included Thomas Muntzer

(d. 1525), Caspar Schwenckfeld (d. 1561), Michael Servetus (d. 1553), and Lelio Sozzini (d. 1562).

3.8 DOCTRINES

The Reformation produced much thought and writing about the beliefs of Christianity. Most of the major divisions of the Western church took differing positions on these matters of doctrine. Some thinkers, such as Martin Bucer, a reformer in Strasbourg, believed many things, such as the ring in the marriage ceremony, were "things indifferent" – Christians could differ in their beliefs on such issues – but with the increasing rigidity of various churches, such views did not dominate.

The role of the Bible was emphasized by Protestants while Catholics included the traditions developed by the church during the Middle Ages, as well as papal pronouncements.

Catholics retained the medieval view about the special nature and role of clergy while Protestants emphasized the 'priesthood of all believers,' which meant all individuals were equal before God. Protestants sought a clergy that preached.

Church governance varied widely:

1) Catholics retained the medieval hierarchy of believers, priests, bishops, and pope.

2) Anglicans rejected the authority of the pope and substituted the monarch as the Supreme Governor of the church.

3) Lutherans rejected the authority of the pope but kept bishops.

RELIGIOUS SITUATION IN 1560

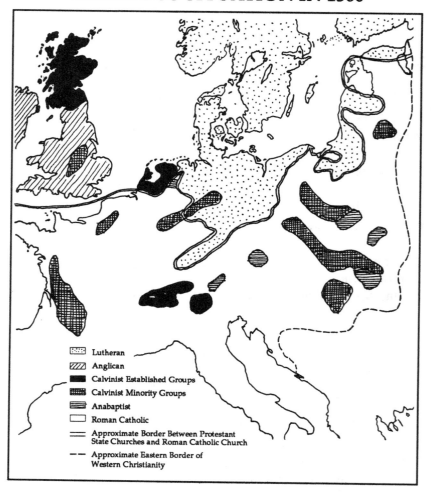

Lutheran
Anglican
Calvinist Established Groups
Calvinist Minority Groups
Anabaptist
Roman Catholic
Approximate Border Between Protestant
State Churches and Roman Catholic Church
Approximate Eastern Border of
Western Christianity

4) Most Calvinists governed their church by ministers and a group of elders, a system called Presbyterianism.

5) Anabaptists rejected most forms of church governance in favor of congregational democracy.

Most Protestants denied the efficacy of some or all of the sacraments of the medieval church. The issue which most divided the various churches came to be the one called by various names: the Eucharist, the mass, the Lord's supper, the communion:

Transubstantiation. The bread and wine retain their outward appearances but the substances are transformed into the body and blood of Christ; this was a Catholic doctrine.

Consubstantiation. Nothing of the bread and wine is changed but the believer realizes the presence of Christ in the bread and wine – a piece of iron thrust into the fire does not change its composition but still has a differing quality; this was a Lutheran doctrine.

Other views included ones that the event was a symbolic one, utilizing the community of believers. It served as a memorial to the actions of Christ, or was a thanksgiving for God's grant of salvation.

The means of obtaining salvation differed:

1) Living the life according to Christian beliefs and participating in the practices of the church – good words; this was Catholic doctrine.

2) Justification by faith – salvation cannot be earned and a good life is the fruit of faith; this was a Lutheran doctrine.

3) Predestination – salvation is known only to God but a good life can be some proof of predestined salvation; this was a Calvinist doctrine.

Relation of the church to the state also differed:

1) The church should control and absorb the state (Catholic and Calvinist). When God is seen as ruling the society, this is a theocracy.

2) The state controls the church (Lutheran and Anglican).

3) The church ignores the state (Anabaptist).

3.9 RESULTS

By 1560, attitudes were hardening and political rulers understood the benefits and disadvantages of religion, be it Catholic or Protestant. The map of Europe and its religions did not change much after 1560.

Political rulers, be they monarchs or city councils, gained power over and at the expense of the church. The state thereafter could operate as an autonomous unit.

Religious enthusiasm was rekindled. While most of the reforms came from the political and religious leadership of the societies involved, the general populus eventually gained enthusiasm – an enthusiasm lacking in religious belief since far back into the Middle Ages.

All aspects of Western Christianity undertook to remedy the abuses which had contributed to the Reformation. Simony, pluralism, immoral or badly educated clergy were all attacked and, by the seventeenth century, considerably remedied.

Protestantism, by emphasizing the individual believer's direct contact with God, rather than through the intermediary of the church, contributed to the growth of individualism.

Thinkers have attempted to connect religious change with economic developments, especially the appearance of capitalism. Karl Marx, a nineteenth-century philosopher and social theorist, believed that capitalism, which emphasized hard work, thrift, and the use of reason rather than tradition, led to the development of Protestantism, a type of Christianity he thought especially attractive to the middle class who were also the capitalists.

Max Weber, a later nineteenth-century sociologist, reversed the argument and believed that Protestantism, especially Calvinism, with its emphasis on predestination, led to great attention being paid to the successes and failures of this world as possible signs of future salvation. Such attention, and the attendant hard work, furthered the capitalist spirit.

Most writers today accept neither view but believe Protestantism and capitalism are related; however too many other factors are involved to make the connection clear or easy.

CHAPTER 4

THE WARS OF RELIGION

4.1 THEMES

The period from approximately 1560 to 1648 witnessed continuing warfare, primarily between Protestants and Catholics. Though religion was not the only reason for the wars – occasionally Catholics and Protestants were allies – religion was the dominant cause of the bloodshed. In the latter half of the sixteenth century, the fighting was along the Atlantic seaboard between Calvinists and Catholics; after 1600, the warfare spread to Germany where Calvinists, Lutherans, and Catholics fought.

4.2 WARFARE

4.2.1 *Effects of Gunpowder*

Cannons became effective and therefore elaborate and expensive fortifications of cities were required. Long sieges became necessary to capture a city.

The infantry, organized in squares of three thousand men and armed with pikes and muskets, made the cavalry charge obsolete.

4.2.2 Discipline

Greater discipline and control of armies were required to sustain a siege or train the infantry. An army once trained would not be disbanded due to the expense of retraining. The order of command and modern ranks appeared, as did uniforms.

The better discipline permitted commanders to attempt more actions on the battlefield, so more soldiers were necessary. Armies grew from the 40,000 of the Spanish army of 1600 to 400,000 in the French army at the end of the seventeenth century.

4.2.3 War and Destruction

Devastation of the enemy's lands became the rule. Armies, mostly made up of mercenaries, lived by pillage when not paid and often were not effectively under the control of the ruler employing them. Peasants, after such devastation and torture to reveal their valuables, left farming and turned to banditry.

4.3 THE CATHOLIC CRUSADE

4.3.1 Philip II (1556 – 98)

The territories of Charles V, the Holy Roman Emperor, were divided in 1556 between Ferdinand, Charles' brother, and Philip, Charles' son. Ferdinand received Austria, Hungary, Bohemia and the title of Holy Roman Emperor. Philip received Spain, Milan, Naples, the Netherlands, and the New World.

Both parts of the Hapsburg family cooperated in international matters.

Philip was a man of severe personal habits, deeply religious, and a hard worker. Solemn (it is said he only laughed once in his life, when the report of the St. Bartholomew's Day massacre reached him) and reclusive (he built the Escorial outside Madrid as a palace, monastery and eventual tomb), he devoted his life and the wealth of Spain to making Europe Catholic. It was Philip, not the pope, who led the Catholic attack on Protestants. The pope and the Jesuits, however, did participate in Philip's efforts.

4.3.2 *Sources of the Power of Philip II*

The gold and silver of the New World flowed into Spain, especially following the opening of the silver mines at Potesi in Peru.

Spain dominated the Mediterranean following a series of wars led by Philip's half-brother, Don John, against Moslem (largely Turkish) forces. Don John secured the Mediterranean for Christian merchants with a naval victory over the Turks at Lepanto off the coast of Greece in 1571.

Portugal was annexed by Spain in 1580 following the death of the king without a clear successor. This gave Philip the only other large navy of the day as well as Portuguese territories around the globe.

4.3.3 *Nature of the Struggle*

Calvinism was spreading in England, France, the Netherlands, and Germany. Calvinists supported each other, often disregarding their countries' borders.

England was ruled by two queens, Mary (1553 – 58), who married Philip II, and then Elizabeth (1558 – 1603), while three successive kings of France from 1559 to 1589 were influenced by their mother, Catherine de' Medici. Women rulers were a novelty in European politics.

Monarchs attempted to strengthen their control and the unity of their countries, a process which nobles often resisted.

4.4   CIVIL WAR IN FRANCE

4.4.1 *Background*

Francis I (1515 – 47) obtained control of the French church, when he signed the Concordat of Bologna with the pope, and therefore had no incentive to encourage Protestantism.

With the signing of the Treaty of Cateau-Cambresis in 1559, the struggles of the Hapsburgs and Valois ended, leaving the French with no fear of outside invasion for a while.

John Calvin was a Frenchman and Geneva was near France, so Calvinist ideas spread in France, especially among the nobility. French Calvinists were sometimes called Huguenots.

Three noble families, – Bourbon, Chatillon, and Guise – sought more power and attempted to dominate the monarchs after 1559. Partly due to politics, the Bourbons and Chatillons became Calvinists.

When Henry II (1547 – 59) died as a result of injuries sustained in a tournament, he was succeeded, in succession, by his three sons (Francis II, 1559 – 60, Charles IX 1560 – 74, Henry III 1571 – 89), each influenced by their mother, Catherine de' Medici (1519 – 89), and often controlled by one of the noble families. Though the Monarch was always Catholic until 1589, each king was willing to work with Calvinists or Catholics if it would give him more power and independence.

4.4.2 The Wars

A total of nine civil wars occurred from 1562 to 1589. The wars became more brutal as killing of civilians supplanted military action.

The St. Bartholomew's Day Massacre on August 24, 1572, was planned by Catherine de' Medici and resulted in the deaths of 20,000 Huguenots. The pope had a medal struck celebrating the event and the king of Spain, Philip II, laughed when told of the massacre.

As a result of St. Bartholomew's Day and other killings, Protestants throughout Europe feared for their future.

Several important figures were assassinated by their religious opponents, including two kings (Henry III and Henry IV). The two leading members of the Guise family were killed at the instigation of the king, Henry III, in 1588.

Spain intervened with troops to support the Catholics in 1590.

4.4.3 Henry of Navarre (1589 – 1610)

A Calvinist and member of the Bourbon family, Henry of Navarre became king in 1589 when Henry III was assassinated. Personally popular, Henry began to unite France but was unable to conquer or control Paris, center of Catholic strength. In 1593 he converted to Catholicism saying "Paris is worth a mass."

In this respect, he was a *politique*, more interested in political unity than religious uniformity.

In 1589 Henry issued the Edict of Nantes which permitted Huguenots to worship publicly, to have access to the universities and to public office, and to maintain fortified towns in France to protect themselves. The Edict was not a recognition of the advantages of religious tolerance so much as it was a truce in the religious wars.

4.5   THE REVOLT OF THE NETHERLANDS

The Netherlands was a group of seventeen provinces clustered around the mouth of the Rhine and ruled by the king of Spain. Each province had a tradition of some independence and each elected a *stadholder*, a man who provided military leadership when necessary. The stadholder often was an important noble and often became the most important politician in the province.

Since the Middle Ages the Netherlands had included many cities dominated by wealthy merchants. By 1560 the cities housed many Calvinists, including some who had fled from France.

Philip II, king of Spain, sought to impose a more centralized government on the Netherlands and a stronger Catholic church, following the decrees of the Council of Trent, on the inhabitants. Philip's efforts provoked resistance by some nobles, led by William of Orange (1533 – 84), called "the Silent" because he discussed his political plans with very few people. An agreement and pledge to resist, called the Compromise of 1564 and signed by people throughout the provinces, led to rebellion.

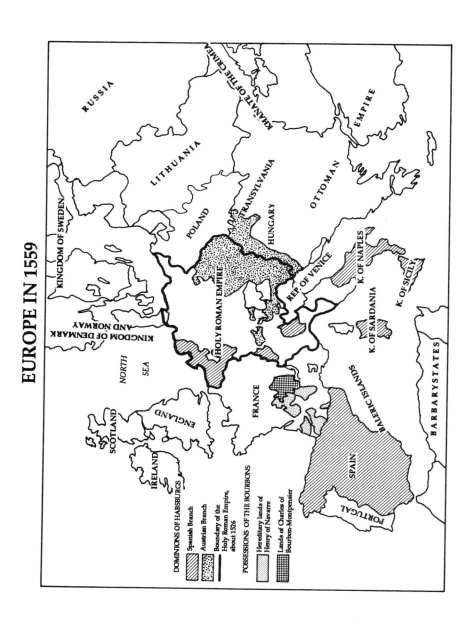

EUROPE IN 1559

DOMINIONS OF HABSBURGS

Spanish Branch

Austrian Branch

Boundary of the
Holy Roman Empire,
about 1526

POSSESSIONS OF THE BOURBONS

Hereditary lands of
Henry of Navarre

Lands of Charles of
Bourbon-Montpensier

RUSSIA

KINGDOM OF SWEDEN

LITHUANIA

POLAND

TRANSYLVANIA

HUNGARY

KHANATE OF THE CRIMEA

OTTOMAN

EMPIRE

REP. OF VENICE

K. OF NAPLES

K. OF SICILY

K. OF SARDANIA

KINGDOM OF DENMARK
AND NORWAY

NORTH

SEA

SCOTLAND

IRELAND

ENGLAND

FRANCE

HOLY ROMAN EMPIRE

BALERIC ISLANDS

SPAIN

PORTUGAL

BARBARY STATES

48

Philip sent the Duke of Alva (1508 – 1583) with 20,000 soldiers to suppress the rebellion. Alva established the Council of Troubles (called the Council of Blood by its opponents) which executed several thousand Calvinists as heretics. Alva also imposed new taxes, including a sales tax of 10%. Most significantly, the Inquisition was established.

The resistance to Alva included groups of sailors, called Sea Beggars, and the opening of the dykes to frustrate the marches of the Spanish armies. In 1576 the Spanish army, unpaid, sacked Antwerp, an event called the Spanish Fury and which destroyed Antwerp's commercial supremacy in the Netherlands.

The Calvinist northern provinces and the Catholic southern provinces united in 1576 in the Pacification of Ghent, but were unable to cooperate and broke apart into two religious groups: the Calvinist Union of Utrecht (approximately modern day Netherlands) and the Catholic Union of Arras (approximately modern day Belgium).

International attention was attracted when a son of Catherine de' Medici attempted to become the leader of the revolt and when the English sent troops and money to support the rebels after 1585.

The Spanish were driven out of the northern Netherlands in the 1590's, and the war ended in 1609, though official independence was not recognized by Spain until 1648. Thereafter, the independent northern provinces, dominated by the province of Holland, were called the United Provinces and the southern provinces, ruled by the king of Spain, the Spanish Netherlands.

4.6 ENGLAND AND SPAIN

4.6.1 *Mary* (1553 – 58)

The daughter of Henry VIII and Katherine of Aragon, Mary sought to make England Catholic. She executed many Protestants, earning her the name "Bloody Mary" by her opponents.

To escape persecution, many of the English went into exile on the Continent where, settling in Frankfort, Geneva, and elsewhere, they learned more radical Protestant ideas.

Cardinal Pole (1500 – 58) was one of Mary's advisers and symbolized the subordination of England to the pope.

Mary married Philip II, king of Spain, and organized her foreign policy around Spanish interests. They had no children.

4.6.2 *Elizabeth* (1558 – 1603)

A Protestant, though one of unknown beliefs, Elizabeth achieved a religious settlement between 1559 and 1563 which left England with a church governed by bishops and practicing Catholic rituals, but maintaining a Calvinist doctrine. This was seen as a *via media* – a middle way between extremes – by its supporters, or an impossible compromise of Protestantism and Catholicism by its opponents.

Puritans sought to purify the English church of the remnants of its medieval heritage and, though suppressed by Elizabeth's government, were not condemned to death.

Catholics, who sought to return the English church to an allegiance to the pope, participated in several rebellions and plots. Mary, Queen of Scots, had fled to England from Scotland in 1568 after alienating the nobles there and was, in Catholic eyes, the legitimate queen of England. Several plots and rebellions to put Mary on the throne led to her execution in 1587.

Elizabeth was formally excommunicated by the pope in 1570. A *politique* interested in the advancing English nation, Elizabeth did not "make windows into men's souls".

In 1588, as part of his crusade and to stop England from supporting the rebels in the Netherlands, Philip II sent the Armada, a fleet of over 125 ships, to convey troops from the Netherlands to England as part of a plan to make England Catholic. The Armada was defeated by a combination of superior English naval tactics and a wind which made it impossible for the Spanish to accomplish their goal.

Peace between Spain and England was signed in 1604. England remained Protestant and an opponent of Spain as long as Spain remained a world power.

4.7   THE THIRTY YEARS' WAR

4.7.1 *Background*

Calvinism was spreading throughout Germany. The Peace of Augsberg, which settled the disputes between Lutherans and Catholics in 1555, had no provision for Calvinists. Lutherans gained more territories through conversions and often took control of previously church states – a violation of the Peace Augsburg. A Protestant alliance under the leadership of the Calvinist ruler of the Palatinate opposed a Catholic League led by the ruler of Bavaria.

4.7.2 *The Bohemian Period* (1618 – 25)

The Bohemians rejected a Hapsburg as their king in favor

of the Calvinist ruler of Palatinate, Frederick. They threw two Hapsburg officials out a window – the "defenestration of Prague."

Frederick's army was defeated at White Mountain in 1620, Bohemia was made Catholic, and the Spanish occupied Frederick's Palatinate.

4.7.3 *The Danish Period* (1625 – 29)

The army of Ferdinand, the Holy Roman Emperor, invaded northern Germany and raised fear among Protestants for their religion and local rulers for their political rights. Christian IV (1588 – 1648), king of Denmark, led an army into Germany in defense of Protestants but was easily defeated. After defeating Christian, the Holy Roman Emperor sought to recover all church lands secularized since 1552 and establish a strong Hapsburg presence in northern Germany.

4.7.4 *The Swedish Period* (1629 – 35)

Gustavus Adolphus (1611 – 32), king of Sweden, supported by money from France and the United Provinces who wanted the Hapsburgs defeated, invaded Germany in defense of Protestantism. Sweden stopped the Hapsburg cause in the battle of Breitenfeld in 1630, but Gustavus Adolphus was killed at the battle of Lutzen in 1632.

4.7.5 *The Swedish-French Period* (1635 – 48)

France, guided by Cardinal Richelieu (1585 – 1642), supplied troops in Germany as the war became part of a bigger war between France and Spain.

4.7.6 *Treaty of Westphalia* (1648)

The presence of ambassadors from all the belligerents and many other countries made settlement of nearly all disputes possible. Only the French-Spanish war continued, ending in 1659.

The principles of the Peace of Augsburg were reasserted, but with Calvinists included. The pope's rejection of the treaty was ignored.

The independence of the United Provinces from the king of Spain and the Swiss Confederacy from the Holy Roman Empire was recognized. Individual German states, numbering over three hundred, obtained nearly complete independence form the Holy Roman Empire.

4.7.7 *Miscellaneous*

Not all issues were ones of Protestants versus Catholics. The Lutheran ruler of Saxony joined the Catholics in the attack on Frederick at White Mountain and the leading general for the Holy Roman Emperor, Ferdinand, was Albrecht of Wallenstein, a Protestant.

The war brought great destruction to Germany, leading to a decline in population of perhaps one-third, more in some areas. Germany remained divided and without a strong government until the nineteenth century.

4.8   RESULTS

After 1648, warfare, though often with religious elements, would not be primarily for religious goals.

The Catholic crusade to reunite Europe failed, largely due to the efforts of the Calvinists. The religious distribution of Europe has not changed significantly since 1648.

Nobles, resisting the increasing power of the state, usually dominated the struggle. France, then Germany, fell apart due to the wars. France was reunited in the seventeenth century; Germany was not.

In most political entities, politiques, such as Elizabeth I of England and Henry IV of France, who sought more to keep the state united than to insure that a single religion dominated, came to control politics.

The branches of the Hapsburg family, the Austrian and the Spanish, continued to to cooperate in international affairs. Spain, though a formidable military power until 1648, began a decline which ended its role as a great power of Europe.

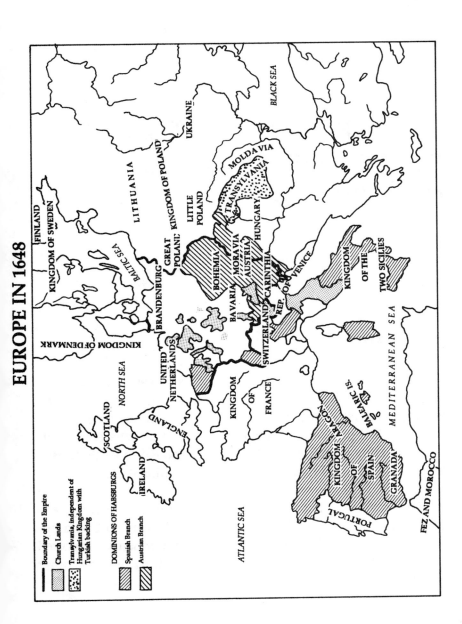

EUROPE IN 1648

Boundary of the Empire

Church Lands

Transylvania, independent of
Hungarian Kingdom with
Turkish backing

DOMINIONS OF HABSBURGS

Spanish Branch

Austrian Branch

BLACK SEA

UKRAINE

FINLAND

KINGDOM OF SWEDEN

LITHUANIA

MOLDAVIA

KINGDOM OF POLAND

GREAT POLAND

LITTLE POLAND

TRANSYLVANIA

HUNGARY

BRANDENBURG

BOHEMIA

MORAVIA

AUSTRIA

BAVARIA

CARINTHIA

REP. OF VENICE

KINGDOM OF THE TWO SICILIES

BALTIC SEA

KINGDOM OF DENMARK

NORTH SEA

UNITED NETHERLANDS

SWITZERLAND

SCOTLAND

ENGLAND

IRELAND

KINGDOM OF FRANCE

BALEARIC IS.

MEDITERRANEAN SEA

ATLANTIC SEA

KINGDOM OF SPAIN

GRANADA

PORTUGAL

FEZ AND MOROCCO

CHAPTER 5

THE GROWTH OF THE STATE AND THE AGE OF EXPLORATION

5.1   THEMES

In the seventeenth century the political systems of the countries of Europe began dividing into two types, absolutist and constitutionalist. While no country typified either type and all countries had part of both, the countries can be separated. England, the United Provinces, and Sweden moved towards constitutionalism, while France was adopting absolutist ideas.

Overseas exploration, begun in the fifteenth century, expanded as the wealth of the New World flowing to Spain became apparent to the rest of Europe. Governments supported such activity in order to gain wealth as well as preempt other countries.

5.2 DEFINITIONS

Constitutionalism meant rules, often unwritten, defining and limiting government. Seeking to enhance the liberty of the individual as well as the individual as a person were goals; in this manner constitutionalism shaded over into Liberalism. Constitutional regimes usually had some means of group decision making, such as a parliament, but a constitutional government need not be a democracy and usually was not. Consent of the governed provided the basis for the legitimacy of the regime, its acceptance by its subject.

Asbolutism emphasized the role of the state and its fulfillment of some specific purpose, such as nationalism, religion, or the glory of the monarch. The usual form of government of an absolutist regime was, in the seventeenth century, kingship, which gained its legitimacy from the notion of divine right or the traditional assumption of power.

Nobles and bourgeoisie, depending on the country, provided the chief opposition to the increasing power of the state. In constitutionalist states, they often obtained control of the state, while in absolutist states they became servants of the state.

5.3 POLITICAL THOUGHT

The collapse of governments during the wars of religion and the subjection of one religious group to the government of another stimulated thought about the nature of politics and political allegiances. The increasing power of the monarchs raised questions about the nature and extent of that power.

Both Protestants and Catholics developed theories of resistance to a government:

1) Luther and Calvin had disapproved of revolt or rebellion against government.

2) John Knox's *Blast of the Trumpet Against the Terrible Regiment of Women* (1558) approved rebellion against a heretical ruler. His text was directed against Mary, Queen of Scotland.

3) In France, Huguenot writers, stimulated by the St. Bartholomew Day's Massacre, developed the idea of a covenant (contract) between people and God and between subjects and monarch. If the monarch ceased to observe the covenant, the purpose of which was to honor God, the representatives of the people (usually the nobles or others in an assembly of some sort) could resist the monarch.

4) Catholic writers, such as Robert Bellarmine, saw the monarch given authority, especially religious authority, by God. With the pope as God's deputy on earth, the pope could dispose of a monarch who put people's souls in jeopardy by wrong beliefs.

Jean Bodin (1530 – 96), in response to the chaos of France during the civil wars, developed the theory of sovereignty. He believed that in each country one power or institution must be strong enough to make everyone else obey; otherwise chaos results from the conflicts of institutions or groups of equal power. Bodin provided the theoretical basis for absolutist states.

Resistance to the power of monarchs was based upon claims to protect local customs, "traditional liberties" and "the ancient constitution." Nobles and towns appealed to the medieval past when sovereignty had been shared by kings, nobles, and other institutions.

The struggles in the seventeenth century produced varying results. At the extremes, an absolutist country was ruled by a monarch from whom all power followed while a constitutional country would limit government power and have a means of determining the will of the people, or at least some of them:

1) The French king dispensed with all representative institutions, dominated the nobility, and ruled directly.

2) The nobles controlled the English government through the representative institution of Parliament .

3) In Germany, various components of the Holy Roman Empire defeated the Emperor and governed themselves independently of him.

5.4   ENGLAND

5.4.1   *Problems Facing English Monarchs*

Religion. The English church was a compromise of Catholic practices and Protestant beliefs and was criticized by both groups. The monarchs, after 1620, gave leadership of the church to men with Arminian beliefs.

Arminius (1560 – 1609), a Dutch theologian, had changed Calvinist beliefs so as to modify slightly the emphasis on predestination. English Arminians also sought to emphasize the role of ritual in church services and enjoyed the "beauty of holiness," which their opponents took to be too Catholic. William Laud (1573 – 1645), Archbishop of Canterbury, accelerated the growth of Arminianism.

Opponents to this shift in belief were called Puritans, a term that covered a wide range of beliefs and people. To escape the church in England, many Puritans began moving to the New World, especially Massachusetts. Both James I and Charles I made decisions which, to Puritans, favored Catholics too much.

Finance. Inflation and Elizabeth's wars left the government short of money. Contemporaries blamed the shortage on the extravagance of the courts of James I and Charles I. James I sold titles of nobility in an effort to raise money but annoyed the nobles with older titles as well as debasing the entire idea of nobility.

The monarchs lacked any substantial source of income and had to obtain the consent of a Parliament to levy a tax. The monarchs would face numerous concerns in dealing with a parliamentary body:

1) A Parliament only met when the monarch summoned it. Though Parliaments had existed since the Middle Ages, a Parliament never met for a long period of time.

2) Parliaments consisted of nobles and gentry with a few merchants and lawyers.

3) The men in a Parliament usually wanted the government to remedy grievances as part of the agreement to a tax.

4) In 1621, the power to impeach governmental servants was first used (since the Middle Ages) by a Parliament to eliminate men who had offended members of Parliament.

The Counties. The forty English counties had a tradition of much local independence. The major landowners – the nobles and the gentry – controlled the counties and resented central government interference.

5.4.2 *James I (1603 – 25)*

James ended the war with Spain and avoided any other entanglements, despite the problem that the Thirty Years' War in Germany involved his son-in-law, the ruler of the Palatinate and a Protestant hero. The Earl of Somerset and then the Duke of Buckingham served as favorites for the king, doing much of the work of government and dealing with suitors for royal actions.

5.4.3 *Charles I (1625 – 49)*

Henrietta Maria, a sister of the king of France and a Catholic, became his queen.

Charles stumbled into wars with both Spain and France during the late 1620's. A series of efforts to raise money for the wars led to confrontations with his opponents in Parliaments:

1) A "forced loan" was collected from taxpayers with the promise it would be repaid when a tax was voted by a Parliament.

2) Soldiers were billeted in subjects' houses during the wars.

3) People were imprisoned for resisting these royal actions.

4) In 1626, the Duke of Buckingham was nearly impeached

because of his monopoly of royal offices and his exclusion of others from power.

5) In 1628, Parliament passed the Petition of Right which declared illegal the royal actions in connection with the loans and billeting.

Charles ruled without calling a Parliament during the 1630's. A policy of "thorough" – strict efficiency and much central government activity – was followed. Money was raised by discovering old forms of taxation:

1) A medieval law which required all landowners with a certain amount of wealth to become knights was used to fine those who had not been knighted.

2) All counties were forced to pay money to outfit ships – "ship money" – which had previously been the obligation only of coastal counties.

5.4.4 *Breakdown*

Charles, with the help of the Archbishop Laud, attempted to impose English rituals and the English prayer book on the Scottish church. The Scots revolted and invaded northern England with an army.

To pay for his own army Charles called the Short Parliament, but was not willing to remedy any grievances or changes his policies. In response, the Parliament did not vote any taxes. Charles called another Parliament, the Long Parliament, which attacked his ministers, challenged his religious policies, and refused to trust him with money.

Archbishop Laud and the Earl of Strafford, the two architects of "thorough," were driven from power. The courts of

Star Chamber and High Commission, which had been used to prosecute Charles' opponents, were abolished. When the Irish revolted, Parliament would not let Charles raise an army to suppress them as it was feared he would use the army against his English opponents. John Pym (1584 – 1643) emerged as a leader of the king's opponents in Parliament.

5.4.5 *Civil War*

In August, 1642, Charles abandoned hope of negotiating with his opponents and declared war against them. Charles' supporters were called royalists or Cavaliers. His opponents were called Parliamentarians or Roundheads because among them were London apprentices who wore their hair cut short.

Historians differ on whether to call this struggle the Puritan Revolution, the English Civil Wars, or the Great Rebellion. The issues which precipitated the war were religious differences and how much authority Charles should have in the government.

Charles was defeated. His opponents had allied with the Scots who still had an army in England. Additionally, the New Model Army, with its general Oliver Cromwell (1599 – 1658), was superior to Charles' army.

With the collapse of government, new religious and political groups, such as Levellers, Quakers, and Ranters, appeared.

Following the defeat of Charles, his opponents attempted to negotiate a settlement with him but, with that failing, he was executed on January 30, 1649, and England became a republic for the next eleven years.

The search for a settlement continued until 1689, when the nobles, gentry, and merchants, acting through Parliament, controlled the government and the monarchy.

5.5   FRANCE

5.5.1   *Problems Facing the French Monarchs*

Provincial Autonomy. The regions of France long had a large measure of independence, and local parliaments could refuse to enforce royal laws. The centralization of all government proceeded by replacing local authorities with intendants, civil servants who reported to the king.

Religion. The Huguenots, as a result of the Edict of Nantes, had separate rights and powers, a state within the state. All efforts to unify France under one religion (Catholicism) faced both internal resistance from the Huguenots and the difficulty of dealing with Protestant powers abroad.

Rulers. By 1650, France had been ruled by only one competent adult monarch since 1559. Louis XIII came to the throne at age 9 and Louis XIV at the age of 5. The mothers of both kings, Maria de' Medici and Anne of Austria, governed until the boys were of age. Both queens relied on chief ministers to help govern: Cardinal Richelieu (1585 – 1642) and Cardinal Mazarin (1602 – 61).

5.5.2   *Henry IV (1589 – 1610)*

Henry relied on the duke of Sully (1560 – 1641), the first of a series of strong ministers in the seventeenth century. Sully and Henry increased the involvement of the state in the economy, acting on a theory known as mercantilism.

Monopolies on the production of gunpowder and salt were developed. Only the government could operate mines. A canal was begun to connect the Mediterranean to the Atlantic.

5.5.3   Louis XIII (1610 – 43)

Cardinal Richelieu, first used by Louis' mother, became the real power in France. Foreign policy was difficult because of the problems of religion.

Due to the weakness of France after the wars of religion, Maria de' Medici concluded a treaty with Spain in 1611. In order to keep the Hapsburgs from gaining ascendancy in Germany, Richelieu supplied troops and money to Gustavus Adolphus, a Lutheran, after 1631.

The unique status of the Huguenots was reduced by warfare and the Peace of Alais (1629) when their separate armed cities were eliminated.

The nobility was reduced in power by constant attention to the laws and imprisoning offenders.

5.5.4   Breakdown

Cardinal Mazarin governed because Louis XIV (1643 – 1715) was a minor. During the *Fronde* from 1649 to 1652 the nobility controlled Paris, drove Louis XIV and Mazarin from the city, and attempted to run the government. Noble ineffectiveness, the memories of the chaos of the wars of religion, and the anarchy convinced most people that a strong king was preferable to a warring nobility. The lack of impact of the movement was symbolized by the name of the Fronde, which meant a slingshot used by children to shoot rocks at carriages but which caused no real damage.

5.5.5 *Absolutism*

By 1652, the French people were willing to accept, and the French monarchy had developed the tools to implement, a strong, centralized government. Louis XIV personally saw the need to increase royal power and his own glory, and dedicated his life to these goals. He steadily pursued a policy of "one king, one law, one faith."

5.6   OTHER CONSTITUTIONAL STATES

5.6.1   *United Provinces*

Politics. The seven provinces sent representatives to an Estates-General which was dominated by the richest provinces, Holland and Zealand, and which had few powers. Each province elected a stadholder, a military leader, and usually all the provinces elected the same man, the head of the house of Orange.

Religion. Calvinism divided when Arminius proposed a theology which reduced the emphasis on predestination. Though the stricter Calvinism prevailed, Arminians had full political and economic rights after 1632, and Catholics and Jews were also tolerated, though with fewer rights.

The merchants, dominating the Estates-General, supported the laxer Arminianism and wanted peace, while the house of Orange adopted the stricter Calvinism and sought a more aggressive foreign policy. In 1619 Jan van Oldenbarenveldt (1547 – 1619), representing the merchants, lost a struggle over the issue of renewing war with Spain to Maurice of Nassau, the head of the house of Orange. Until 1650, Maurice and then William II dominated, and the Dutch supported anti-Hapsburg forces in the Thirty Years' War. The merchants regained power, and Jan de Witt (1625 – 72) set about returning power to the provinces in 1653.

The seventeenth century witnessed tremendous growth in the wealth and economic power of the Dutch. The Bank of Amsterdam, founded in 1609, provided safe and stable control of money, which encouraged investments in many kinds of activities. Amsterdam became the financial center of Europe. The Dutch also developed the largest fleet in Europe devoted to trade, not warfare, and became the dominant trading country.

5.6.2 Sweden

Gustavus Adolphus (1611 – 32) reorganized the government, giving the nobles a dominant role in both the army and the bureaucracy. The central government was divided into five departments, each with a noble at its head. The very capable Axel Oxenstierna (1583 – 1654) dominated this government.

The Riksdag, an assembly of nobles, clergy, townsmen, and peasants, nominally had the highest legislative authority, but real power lay with the nobles and the monarch.

From 1611 to 1650, noble power and wealth greatly increased. In 1650 Queen Christina, who wanted to abdicate and become a Catholic (which eventually she did in 1654), used the power of the Riksdag to coerce the nobles into accepting her designated successor.

As a result of Gustavus Adolphus' military actions the Baltic became a Swedish lake and Sweden became a world power. Swedish economic power resulted from copper mines, the only ones in Europe.

In both the United Provinces and Sweden, the government was dominated by rich and powerful groups which used representative institutions to limit the power of the state and produce non-absolutist regimes.

5.7   EXPLORATIONS AND CONQUESTS

5.7.1   *Motives*

Gold and silver were early and continuing reasons for explorations. Still further, the thrill of exploration explains the actions of many. Spices and other aspects of trade quickly became important, especially in Portuguese trade to the East Indies.

Religion proved to be a particularly strong motivation. To engage in missionary work, Jesuits, including Francis Xavier, appeared in India, Japan, and other areas by 1550. English unhappy with their church moved to North America in the seventeenth century.

5.7.2   *Results*

The wealth, especially the gold and silver of Mexico and Peru, enabled Spain to embark on its military activities. European inflation, which existed prior to the discoveries, was further fueled by the influx of gold and silver.

Disease killed perhaps twenty-five million or eighty percent of the Indians of the Americas. Syphilis appeared in Europe for the first time.

Many foods, such as potatoes and tomatoes, were introduced to Europe.

Europeans began transporting slaves from Africa to the Americas.

A large number of English settled in North America and a smaller number of Spaniards in Central and South America. In other areas, few Europeans lived.

5.7.3 Early Explorations

Portugal. Prince Henry the Navigator (1394 – 1460) supported exploration of the African coastline, largely to seek gold. Bartholomew Dias (1450 – 1500) rounded the southern tip of Africa in 1487. Vasco de Gama (1460 – 1524) reached India in 1498 and, after some fighting, soon established trading ports at Goa and Calicut. Albuquerque (1435 – 1515) helped establish an empire in the Spice Islands after 1510.

Spain. Christopher Columbus (1446 – 1506), seeking a new route to the (East) Indies, discovered the Americas in 1492. Ferdinand Magellan (1480 – 1521) started a voyage which first circumnavigated the globe in 1521 – 22. Conquests of the Aztecs by Hernando Cortes (1485 – 1547) and the Incas by Francisco Pizarro (1470 – 1541) enabled the Spanish to send much gold and silver back to Spain, and began the process of subjugating the American Indians.

In 1494, Spain and Portugal, by the treaty of Tordesillas, divided portions of the world they had newly discovered between themselves.

Other Countries. In the 1490's the Cabots, John (1450 – 98) and Sebastian (1474 – 1557), explored North America and, after 1570, various Englishmen, including Francis Drake (1545 – 96), fought the Spanish around the world. The English also discovered a route to Russia through the White Sea and commenced trading there. Jacques Cartier (1491 – 1557) explored parts of North America for France in 1534.

5.7.4 Early Seventeenth-Century Explorations and Settlements

Governments took an increasing interest in settlements and sought to control them and trading ports from European capitals.

England. The Virginia Company settled Jamestown in the Chesapeake Bay in 1607. Soon tobacco became a major export crop. Catholics were allowed to settle in Maryland after 1632.

The Pilgrims arrived in Massachusetts in 1620. Other settlers of the Massachusetts Bay, chartered by the king in 1629, soon arrived. Between 1630 and 1650, over 20,000 people unhappy with religious developments in England emigrated to Massachusetts.

Various West Indies Islands were also settled.

France. Following Samuel de Champlain's (1567 – 1635) first efforts in 1603, the French explored the St. Lawrence River. Trade, especially for furs, was the goal. The Company of the Hundred Associates, founded in 1627, undertook the development of Canada. The West Indies attracted groups of investors such as the Company of St. Christopher, which was organized in 1626.

Other Countries. The Dutch sent Henry Hudson (d. 1611) to explore North America in 1609 and soon established settlements at New Amsterdam and in the Hudson River valley. The Dutch founded trading centers in the East Indies, the West Indies, and southern Africa. Swedes settled on the Delaware River in North America in 1638.

EARLY EUROPEAN EXPLORATIONS

LINE OF TORDESILLAS TREATY 1494

NORTH AMERICA

ATLANTIC OCEAN

1493

1492

SOUTH AMERICA

PACIFIC OCEAN

1520

1519

EUROPE

ASIA

AFRICA

INDIA

1498

1487

1497

1522

1521

Death of Magellan
(Crew continues voyage)

AUSTRALIA

– – –	Dias
·········	Columbus
–·–·–	Da Gama
———	Magellan

CHAPTER 6

SCIENCE, LEARNING AND SOCIETY

6.1   THEMES

The scientific revolution of the sixteenth and seventeenth centuries replaced religion as the explanation for the occurrences of the physical world. In contrast to religious articles of faith, the approach of science relied on experiment and mathematics. Learning, including the arts, moved away from Renaissance models to emphasize the emotions and individual variations.

While the family as an institution remained unchanged, much of society was transformed by population growth, inflation, and new patterns of landholding, trade, and industry.

6.2   THE SCIENTIFIC REVOLUTION

6.2.1 *Astronomy*

Astronomy, and to a lesser degree physics, first produced the new ways of thought called the scientific revolution.

Middle Ages. The ideas of the ancient Greek Aristotle (384 – 22 B.C.) provided the system of explanations. Aristotle believed the motionless earth occupied the center of the universe, and the sun, planets, and stars revolved around it in circular orbits determined by crystalline spheres. Aristotle's system was further refined by Ptolemy, a second-century astronomer, to make it correspond to the observed movements of the stars and planets.

Nicolaus Copernicus (1473 – 1543). Accepting the Aristotelian idea that the circle is the closest to the perfect figure and the Renaissance belief in simple explanations, Copernicus suggested that the sun was at the center of the universe and that the earth and planets revolved around it in circular orbits. His *On the Revolutions of the Heavenly Spheres* was published in 1543, the year of his death. Copernicus' ideas meant the universe was immense, removed people from occupying the center of the universe to inhabiting a small planet in a vast system, and eliminated distinctions between the earth and the heavens.

Copernicus' views were not immediately accepted because they contradicted the words of the Bible and, as he posited circular orbits for the planets, did not accurately predict their locations.

Tycho Brahe (1546 – 1601). A Danish nobleman, Brahe built the best observatory of his time and collected extensive data on the location of the stars and planets. Brahe did not totally accept Copernicus' views as he believed that the earth still occupied the center of the universe but that the other planets revolved around the sun, which, in turn, revolved around the earth.

Brahe's discovery of a new star in 1572 and the appearance of a comet in 1577 shattered beliefs in an unchanging sky and crystalline spheres.

Johannes Kepler (1571 – 1630). Kepler's reworking of Copernicus' theory and Brahe's observations produced the idea that the planets move around the sun in elliptical, nor circular, orbits. The three new laws of Kepler accurately predicted the movements of the planets and were based on mathematical relationships.

Galileo (1564 – 1642). Galileo discovered four moons of Jupiter using a telescope, a new invention of the time. He also conducted other experiments in physics related to the relationship of movement of objects and the mathematics necessary to describe the movement, such as that of the pendulum.

A propagandist for science, Galileo defended his discoveries and mocked his opponents. The Catholic Church in Italy, where Galileo lived and worked, forced him to recant his views, which demonstrated the conflict of the older religious views and the new scientific approach.

6.2.2 Scientific Methodologies

Francis Bacon (1561 – 1626). The author of *Advancement of Learning* (1605) and an advocate of experimental approaches to knowledge, Bacon formalized empiricism, an approach using inductive reasoning. An Englishman, Bacon himself did few experiments but believed empiricism would produce useful, not only theoretical, knowledge.

Rene Descartes (1596 – 1650). Beginning from basic principles, Descartes believed scientific laws could be found by deductive reasoning. Formulating analytic geometry, Descartes knew that geometry and algebra were related and that equations could describe figures. Later developments merged inductive experimentalism with deductive, mathematical rationalism to produce today's epistemology, the methods to obtain and verify knowledge.

6.2.3 Connections with the Rest of Society

During the Renaissance many universities established the study of mathematics and physics. All the great scientists involved in the changes in astronomy studied at universities.

The demands of the explorers, especially those at sea, for more accurate measurements of the stars increased attention on the details of the heavenly movements.

Warfare, particularly the developing use of artillery, required and permitted explanations involving precise measurements.

Initially, Protestant areas were more hostile than Catholic ones to the new learning, but after Galileo, Catholic authorities led in trying to suppress the new ideas.

6.2.4 Consequences

The new approaches of the scientific method spread to inquiries far beyond astronomy and physics. Many sought new explanations as well as order and uniformity in all aspects of the physical world and society.

William Harvey (1578 – 1657), demonstrated the circulation of blood and the role of the human heart. Thomas Hobbes (1558 – 1679), an English writer on political theory, studied society and, using a few basic premises, described politics in *Leviathan* (1651).

Blaise Pascal (1623 – 62), a French mathematician and scientist, developed several new ideas, including the basis for calculus, but worried about the increasing reliance on science which he believed could not explain the truly important things of life; these could only be perceived by faith. Human beings, which had been at the center of the universe and the central link in the Great Chain of Being, became merely creatures in an unintelligibly vast universe.

Scientists slowly replaced the clergy as the people able to explain the happenings of the physical world. However, few of the discoveries – except for the aids to explorers – had any consequences on the lives of Europeans.

6.3   LITERATURE AND THE ARTS

6.3.1   *Literature*

Cervantes (1647 – 1616). Cervantes, a Spaniard, was a former soldier and slave concerned with the problems of religious idealism. *Don Quixote* (1605) satirized chivalric romances and described a worldly-wise, skeptical peasant (Sancho Panzo) and a mentally unstable religious idealist (Don Quixote).

William Shakespeare (1564 – 1616). Mixing all aspects of English life in the years around 1600 – country, court, Renaissance ideas – Shakespeare wrote tragedies, comedies, histories, and sonnets. Besides a gift for psychological studies of his characters and the timelessness of his themes, Shakespeare used the English language in new ways which permanently altered it.

John Milton (1608 – 1674). Influenced by the Renaissance while travelling in Italy, the Englishman Milton also had strong Puritan religious beliefs. *Paradise Lost* studied the motives of those who reject God. Milton took an active part in the troubles in England from 1640 to 1660 as a secretary to a committee of Parliament.

Michel de Montaigne (1533 – 92). A Frenchman, Montaigne became obsessed with death and the problems it raised. The inventor of the form of the essay, he adopted skepticism, doubting that true knowledge can be obtained, before turning to a belief in the value of individual self-study.

6.3.2 The Arts

Mannerism. Rejecting the balance and calm of Renaissance arts, Mannerists, who dominated painting and sculpture in the latter part of the sixteenth century, emphasized dramatic and emotional qualities. El Greco (1541 – 1614), a Greek who lived in Spain, took Mannerist qualities to the extreme.

Baroque. In the seventeenth century artists attempted to involve the viewer by emphasizing passion and mystery as well as drama. Baroque, which emphasized grandeur, was connected with the Counter Reformation and monarchies, and was found primarily in Catholic countries.

The works of Bernini (1598 – 1680), such as his *David*, capture the appeal to emotion, the sense of tension in the object, and the human energy of their subjects. Rubens (1577 – 1640), painting both religious and secular themes, conveyed the strength and majesty of his subjects.

In music, Monteverdi (1647 – 1643), using many new instruments such as strings and woodwinds, wrote *Orfeo* (1607) and is known as the creator of the opera and the orchestra.

Later in the seventeenth century, architecture, especially that of palaces, displayed the forces of power by adopting baroque forms.

6.4   SOCIETY

6.4.1   *Hierarchy*

A system whereby people, usually as members of groups, are ranked from highest to lowest in terms of power, wealth, or status became the dominant view in the Europe of the sixteenth and seventeenth centuries.

Two major hierarchies existed: the countryside and the cities. Rural hierarchy consisted of landlords, peasants, landless laborers. Urban hierarchy was comprised of merchants, artisans, laborers. Clergy, lawyers, teachers, and civil servants fit somewhat awkwardly in both hierarchies.

New and expanding groups relied on education or wealth to join older groups. People seeking to join the aristocracy often sought education as a means of acquiring noble status and behavior. Wealth permitted an artisan to become a merchant or, after a generation or two, a rich peasant to become a noble. The advantages of being in a higher group, besides the status, could include separate taxes and exemption from some taxes.

Social mobility – the changing from one group to another – was not accepted in the writings of the day but did occur, though it was very hard to measure.

6.4.2   *Demography*

Exact numbers concerning population are not possible, as complete censuses do not exist. Following the Black Death and its repeated appearances in the fourteenth century, the population remained stagnant. Population began growing again in the sixteenth century and continued its upward climb until about 1650 when it levelled off for another century. The population of Europe nearly doubled between 1500 and 1650.

The population (very approximate) of some European countries in 1650 can be estimated at the following levels:

England	5.5 million
France	18.0 million
Holy Roman Empire	11.0 million
Italian peninsula	12.0 million
Spain	5.2 million
Sweden	1.5 million
United Provinces	1.5 million

Cities grew much faster than the population as a whole as people migrated from the countryside. London grew from 50,000 in 1500 to 200,000 in 1650. Cities contained perhaps 10 to 20 percent of the total population of Europe.

Though historians and demographers are not certain, population probably grew because of slight declines in the average age of marriage and better nutrition, not better medicine.

6.4.3 The Family

The usual family consisted of parents and children, the nuclear family. A baby had a twenty-five percent chance of sur-

EUROPEAN CITIES IN 1600

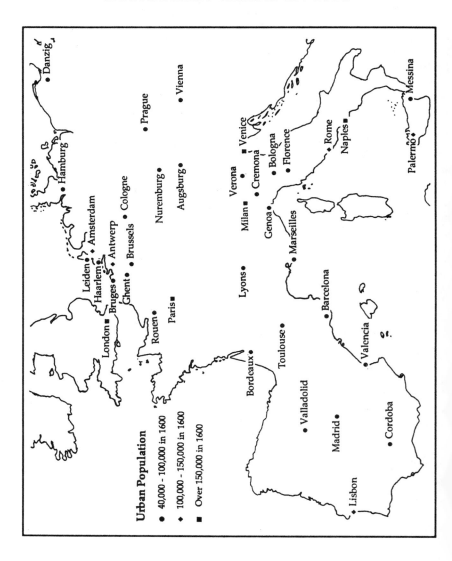

Urban Population
- 40,000 - 100,000 in 1600
♦ 100,000 - 150,000 in 1600
■ Over 150,000 in 1600

viving to the age of one, a fifty percent chance of surviving to the age of twenty and a ten percent chance of reaching sixty. The average age of marriage was approximately 27 for men and 25 for women, though the nobility married younger. Few people married early enough or lived long enough to see their grandchildren.

The theory of family relationships, as expressed in sermons and writings, was one of patriarchy with the father and husband responsible for and in command of the rest of the family. The reality of family relationships was more complex and, due to lack of sources, is not clear to historians.

Romantic love did exist, especially after marriage, but historians disagree as to whether it was the dominant element in forming marriages. Women, particularly in urban areas, shared in the work of their artisan and merchant husbands but rarely operated a business on their own.

The family was stable as divorce was very rare.

6.4.4 Witchcraft

Witch-hunting, though found in the late Middle Ages, occurred primarily in the sixteenth and seventeenth centuries. Belief in witches was found among the educated, the religious, the poor – all parts of society.

Historians and anthropologists provide many explanations as to why people believed in witches and why witch-hunting occurred when and where it did. Perhaps people needed a reason when things went badly. Another explanation is that the increased concern with religion as a result of the Reformation focused more attention on the role of the devil in life.

A charge of witchcraft could punish the aberrant, the non-conformist. Repression of sexuality could result in the projection of fears and hopes onto women, who then had to be punished. Though exact numbers are not possible, thousands of witches were executed, with variations of numbers from place to place.

6.4.5 *Food and Diet*

Bread was the staff of life and the chief item in the diet of the laboring classes. Vegetables included peas and beans, as the vegetables from the Americans were not widely used by 1650. Meat and eggs were saved for special occasions except among the richer elements of society. Beverages included beer and wine as milk was considered unhealthy except for the young.

Nobles and the bourgeoisie ate lots of rich meats and fish with cheeses and sweets, but few vegetables or fruit. The English ate better than the rest of Europe, with the peoples of the Mediterranean areas eating the worst.

Local famines were still common as governments lacked the ability to move food from an area of surplus to one of dearth.

6.4.6 *The Economy*

Inflation, sometimes called the price revolution, began around 1500 and continued until about the middle of the seventeenth century. Foodstuffs rose in price tenfold. The rise in population was the primary cause of the inflation as there were more mouths to feed than food available. Another possible cause was the flow of silver from the Americas which increased the amount of money available to buy things.

Farmers sought to increase output as the price of food rose. Land was brought under cultivation, which had been idle since the Black Death of 1348. In England, enclosures, which resulted in fewer people living on the land, produced larger, more efficient farms. In Eastern Europe, landlords turned their lands into large wheat exporting operations and began the process of converting the peasants and laborers into serfs.

Trade and industry. Trade grew, both with the rest of the world and within Europe. Certain areas began to specialize: for example, the lands south and east of the Baltic produced wheat for northwestern Europe. The Dutch fleet dominated European trade.

The textile industry, the chief industry of Europe since the Middle Ages, underwent change. Regional specialization occurred on a larger scale. The putting-out system appeared whereby the industry moved out of the cities into the countryside and the process of production was divided into many steps with different workers doing each step.

6.4.7 Mercantilism

The conscious pursuit by governments of policies designed to increase national wealth, especially of gold, became common in the seventeenth century. The chief aim was to obtain a favorable balance of international payments. Governments sought to create industries in order to avoid importing items.

The Essentials of **HISTORY**

REGISTERED TRADEMARK

REA's **Essentials of History** series offers a new approach to the study of histo that is different from what has been available previously. Compared with conve tional history outlines, the **Essentials of History** offer far more detail, with fuller planations and interpretations of historical events and developments. Compar with voluminous historical tomes and textbooks, the **Essentials of History** offe far more concise, less ponderous overview of each of the periods they cover.

The **Essentials of History** provide quick access to needed information, and v serve as a handy reference source at all times. The **Essentials of History** a prepared with REA's customary concern for high professional quality and stude needs.

UNITED STATES HISTORY

1500 to 1789	From Colony to Republic
1789 to 1841	The Developing Nation
1841 to 1877	Westward Expansion & the Civil War
1877 to 1912	Industrialism, Foreign Expansion & the Progressive Era
1912 to 1941	World War I, the Depression & the New Deal
1941 to 1988	America as a World Power

EUROPEAN HISTORY

1450 to 1648	The Renaissance, Reform- ation & Wars of Religion
1648 to 1789	Bourbon, Baroque & the Enlightenment
1789 to 1848	Revolution & the New European Order
1848 to 1914	Realism & Materialism
1914 to 1935	World War I & Europe in Crisis
1935 to 1988	World War II & the Iron Curtain

WORLD HISTORY

Ancient History (4,500BC to 500AD)
The Emergence of Western Civilization

Medieval History (500 to 1450AD)
The Middle Ages

If you would like more information about any of these books,
complete the coupon below and return it to us or go to your local bookstore.

RESEARCH and EDUCATION ASSOCIATION
61 Ethel Road W. • Piscataway, New Jersey 08854
Phone: (201) 819-8880

Please send me more information about your History ESSENTIALS books.

Name _____

Address _____

City _____ State _____ Zip_____